Chillenden Mill, Kent. Built in 1868, this post mill was rebuilt in 2005 after being blown over in a storm.

Windmills

Martin Watts

A Shire book

Published in 2006 by Shire Publications Ltd,
Cromwell House, Church Street, Princes Risborough,
Buckinghamshire HP27 9AA, UK.
(Website: www.shirebooks.co.uk)

Copyright © 2006 by Martin Watts.
First published 2006.
Shire Album 456. ISBN-10: 0 7478 0653 5.
ISBN-13: 978 0 7478 0653 0.
Martin Watts is hereby identified as the author of this work
in accordance with Section 77 of the Copyright, Designs
and Patents Act 1988.

British Library Cataloguing in Publication Data:
Watts, Martin
Windmills. – (Shire album; 456)
1. Windmills – Great Britain – History
I. Title 621.4′53′0941
ISBN-10: 0 7478 0653 5.

Cover: *John Webb's Mill, Thaxted, Essex.*

ACKNOWLEDGEMENTS

I am indebted to many people, past and present, who have enlivened and informed my interest in mills over a considerable period of time, and to all those mill owners and custodians who have allowed me access to the fascinating historic buildings in their care. In compiling this present introduction to windmills, I am particularly grateful to Luke Bonwick, Mildred Cookson, Roy Gregory, Peter Hill, Simon Hudson, Dave Pearce, Alan Stoyel and James Waterfield, who have all helped with information and illustrations. I am, as ever, grateful to Sue, my wife, for her practical support and constructive criticism throughout and for taking some of the photographs.

Illustrations are taken from material in the author's own collection, with some exceptions, which are acknowledged as follows: Luke Bonwick, page 59; Mildred Cookson, pages 22 (top), 53 (top); Peter Hill, page 48 (bottom); Cadbury Lamb, pages 3, 5 (bottom), 22 (bottom), 28 (bottom), 40 (bottom), 56, 60, 61 (right); Ken Major, page 4 (right); Dave Pearce, page 58; John Spencer, page 20 (bottom); James Waterfield, page 18 (bottom); Jim Woodward-Nutt, page 20 (top).

Printed in Malta by Gutenberg Press Limited, Gudja Road, Tarxien PLA 19, Malta

Contents

The tower mill at Great Bircham, Norfolk, built in 1846 and maintained in working order.

Historical background

The first windmills in Europe were built on both sides of the North Sea and English Channel, in south and east England, Flanders and northern France, and the earliest unambiguous references to mills specifically driven by wind appear in documents dating from the 1180s. While the earliest known windmills in England were all sited to the east of an imaginary line between the Solent and the Tyne, by the end of the thirteenth century they were widespread and were also recorded in south and west Wales. In Scotland, windmills are first mentioned in about the middle of the fifteenth century. These early windmills were built partly to supplement watermills and, in certain parts of Britain, where water power was less readily available owing to the topography and rainfall, to supplant them. While some of the earliest recorded windmills were associated with religious houses and the clergy, they were also built in large numbers by secular landowners and became an important commercial asset on many manors, where their use by unfree tenants was compulsory. It has been estimated that by 1300 there were about ten thousand mills in England, of which about four thousand were windmills. Windmills were primarily used for grinding grain for meal and flour, but later in the Middle Ages they were also used to pump water, for draining land and, from the end of the sixteenth century, to drive machinery for processing raw materials for an increasing number of industrial purposes.

Left: *A fifteenth-century carving of a post mill on a bench-end in the parish church at Thornham, Norfolk.*

Below: *A miller bringing grain to his mill; a sixteenth-century misericord in Bristol Cathedral.*

Windmill types

POST MILLS

It is generally considered that the earliest type of windmill to be built in England was the post mill, a remarkable structure comprising a timber-framed and clad body, or buck, as it is known in East Anglia, containing the gearing and millstones, mounted on a massive vertical post. The weight of the body and machinery is carried by a heavy horizontal crossbeam, the crown tree, which turns on the head of the post. The sails, which rotate in an almost vertical plane, are fixed to the outer end of a timber axle, the windshaft, which is slightly inclined at its inner end, to take some of the weight of the sails into the body of the mill. The body can be rotated through 360 degrees, in order to face the sails squarely into the wind. Access to the working part of the mill is by a ladder, the bottom end of which is lowered to the ground and acts as a stabiliser when the mill is at work, countering the thrust of the wind against the sails. From medieval illustrations it appears that

The remains of Essington post mill, Staffordshire, with the crown tree still perched on top of the post.

Below: *The post mill at Pitstone, Buckinghamshire, owned by the National Trust. contains some timbers that date from the late sixteenth century.*

the earliest post mills were relatively small, cramped structures and contained only a single pair of millstones driven by a pair of gears from the windshaft. Such illustrations and finds made by archaeological excavation further suggest that the substructure – the post and its supporting structure, or trestle – went through a period of development. Some mills had their substructures buried in an earthen mound to increase their stability, before the familiar surviving arrangement, where the post is supported by (usually) four quarterbars and two crosstrees raised on masonry piers above ground level, was arrived at. Some mills that are still standing, for example at Drinkstone, Suffolk, and Madingley, Cambridgeshire, have posts made from oak trees that were felled in the sixteenth century but, as with all engines, parts wear out through use and decay and require replacement to keep the machinery at work, so that the structure and gearing of surviving mills are generally the result of several generations of rebuilding and reuse.

Above: *The trestle of Cromer Mill, Hertfordshire, with the post supported by raking quarterbars and horizontal crosstrees. The timber collar, which carries some of the weight of the mill, is visible at the top of the quarterbars.*

The post of Drinkstone Mill, Suffolk, is made from an oak tree felled c.1586.

By the eighteenth century the timber trestle was often enclosed in a roundhouse, which both protected the timbers from the weather and provided additional storage and working space. In the Midlands roundhouses built of stone or brick were sometimes used to provide additional stability for the body of the mill, some of the weight of which was taken by rollers running on a timber circle, or curb, on top of the masonry wall, as at Dale Abbey, Derbyshire. Some post mills, such as Stevington, Bedfordshire, contain only a single pair of millstones, driven directly from the brakewheel mounted on the windshaft, while others, as at Nutley, East Sussex, have a second pair of stones located towards the rear of the mill body, driven from a second gear, the tail wheel, fixed to the windshaft. An alternative layout was to have two pairs of millstones positioned across the front, or breast, of the mill body, driven from above or below by spur gearing. In East Anglia and south-east England post mills continued to

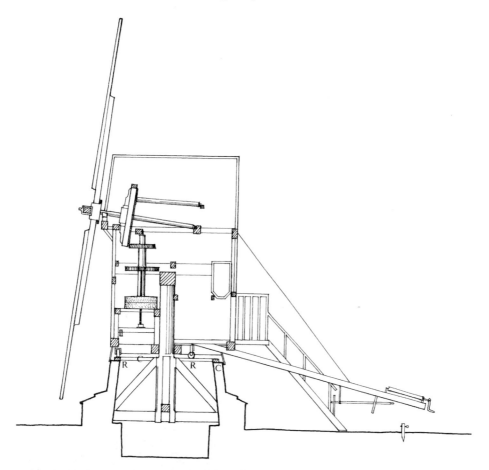

Section through Dale Abbey Mill, Derbyshire, showing how some of the weight of the mill body is taken on rollers, R, which run on a curb, C, on the top of the roundhouse wall.

Section through a small post mill, with a roundhouse enclosing the trestle, at Stevington, Bedfordshire. P is the post and T the crosstrees, which sit on masonry piers, M, incorporated in the walls of the roundhouse, R. The weight of the mill is taken by the crown tree, C, on which the body turns, and the collar, c, at the top of the quarterbars, Q.

The open-trestle post mill at Nutley, East Sussex. The oak post dates from the mid sixteenth century.

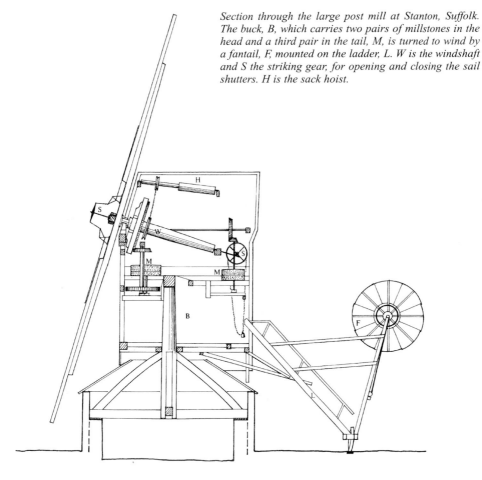

Section through the large post mill at Stanton, Suffolk. The buck, B, which carries two pairs of millstones in the head and a third pair in the tail, M, is turned to wind by a fantail, F, mounted on the ladder, L. W is the windshaft and S the striking gear, for opening and closing the sail shutters. H is the sack hoist.

be built into the nineteenth century, some working with as many as three pairs of millstones. The open-trestle post mill at Chillenden, Kent, was built as late as 1868 and rebuilt in 2005, after being blown down in 2003. The fine white-painted weatherboarded East Anglian post mills, such as those still standing at Saxtead Green, Suffolk, and Aythorpe Roding, Essex, perhaps represent the ultimate development of the post-mill form.

The hollow-post mill, in which the post was bored through its length so that a vertical shaft driven from the brakewheel could pass through and take the drive to the base of the trestle, was developed in the Netherlands for land drainage, perhaps as early as the fourteenth century, but examples appear to have been relatively rare in Britain. The unusual windmill on Wimbledon Common, London, was built as a hollow-post mill in 1817, but its original form was altered when it was restored in 1893.

Aythorpe Roding Mill, Essex. Originally built in 1779, the mill was modernised and a fantail added in the nineteenth century.

The restored former hollow-post mill on Wimbledon Common, London, now houses a windmill museum.

TOWER MILLS

The relative frailty of early post-mill construction, particularly in exposed locations and those parts of Britain where good building timber was in short supply, resulted in the development of a windmill form in which the machinery was enclosed within a masonry tower. The tower wall, either cylindrical or slightly conical in shape, was topped with a timber-framed roof or cap mounted on a curb, so that it could be rotated through 360 degrees, to face the sails to the wind. The earliest known tower mill in England was that erected at Dover Castle in 1294/5, which cost over four times as much to build as a contemporary post mill. Other tower mills followed, but the building accounts that have survived suggest that they were a relatively complex as well as an expensive alternative to post mills and, as carpenters were the dominant craftsmen responsible for the construction of mills during the Middle Ages, tower mills were not generally considered to be a viable economic alternative to post mills until the eighteenth century. There are some interesting exceptions, however. In south-west England a number of windmill towers survive that may be of late-medieval origin, for example at Fowey, Cornwall, and the two towers that stand on the Isle of Portland, Dorset, are marked on an early-seventeenth-century map. Similarly, an early tower mill survives on the Channel Island of Sark. Built at the Seigneur's expense in 1571 and subsequently heightened and refitted, it is the

The tower of a probable medieval windmill at Fowey, Cornwall, which was turned into a folly in the early twentieth century.

The remains of two early-seventeenth-century stone tower mills standing at Easton on the Isle of Portland, Dorset.

southernmost windmill in the British Isles to retain machinery. The use of stone in such locations is not surprising and in Somerset the tradition was for small tower mills, often with only one or two pairs of millstones, which generally replaced post mills from at least the middle of the eighteenth century.

Two unusual tower mills survive in Warwickshire. At Burton Dassett a stone tower known as the Beacon is almost certainly the remains of

The remains of a medieval stone windmill tower at Burton Dassett, Warwickshire.

Ashton Mill, Chapel Allerton, Somerset, a small tower mill built into a mound on which a post mill stood until the mid eighteenth century.

a medieval tower mill, first mentioned in the fourteenth century. A little further north, overlooking the Fosse Way, is the unique seventeenth-century tower mill at Chesterton. Built as a windmill in 1632 for the landowner Sir Edward Peyto, and probably designed by him, Chesterton is an exceptional survival, retaining machinery of early design and construction that drove two pairs of millstones.

Brick was used for building windmill towers from the late seventeenth century, particularly in eastern England, and the design of the tall, conical brick tower mills that first appeared in East Yorkshire in the 1770s probably originated in the Low

Below left: *The tower mill on Sark, Channel Islands. Originally built in 1571, it was heightened and new machinery fitted in the nineteenth century.*

Below right: *The unique Chesterton Mill, Warwickshire, built as a windmill in 1632 and now maintained by Warwickshire County Council.*

The tall brick tower mill at Scopwick, Lincolnshire, built in 1827.

Countries. These mills provided a number of advantages over timber-built post mills and small tower mills, with increased storage capacity and working space. They were also more powerful, sometimes with five or six sails driving three or four pairs of millstones. Many fine examples can still be found in Lincolnshire, for example the Trader Mill at Sibsey, an elegant brick tower mill with six sails, which replaced a post mill in 1877 and was among the last traditional windmills to be built in England.

SMOCK MILLS

The smock mill is really a form of tower mill, rather than a separate windmill type. It is a timber-framed and clad tower, usually octagonal, but occasionally with six, ten or twelve

The six-sailed Trader Mill at Sibsey, Lincolnshire, built in 1877, is maintained in working order by English Heritage.

The smock mill at Lacey Green, Buckinghamshire.

sides, raised on a brick base. The height of the brick base varies from a low plinth, as at Lacey Green, Buckinghamshire, to two storeys, as at Cranbrook, Kent, where the height was necessary to raise the sails clear of the surrounding buildings. Smock mills were probably introduced in the late sixteenth century from the Netherlands, where they were developed for land drainage work. The timber-framed structure had a number of advantages over brick or stone towers, as mills could be prefabricated, taken to site, erected and subsequently dismantled when their work was done. The timber construction was also lighter on unstable ground, such as that recovered by drainage work. Smock mills were adopted most widely in those areas of Britain where a strong timber-framing tradition existed, such as south

Shade Mill, Soham, Cambridgeshire. This photograph, taken before restoration in the 1990s, shows some of the structure of the timber-framed tower.

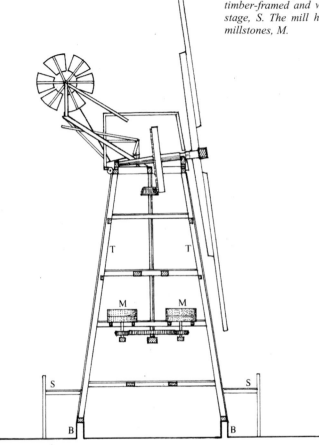

Section through a smock mill, based on that at Stelling Minnis, Kent. B is the brick base, T the timber-framed and weatherboarded tower with a stage, S. The mill has two pairs of underdriven millstones, M.

and south-east England. Smock mills for grinding corn are particularly representative of Kent and also of Cambridgeshire, although there is a notable contrast between their appearances.

Other types of windmill were built, such as composite mills, a hybrid form in which a post-mill body was mounted on a short tower, and horizontal windmills, where the sails turned in a horizontal plane, but no complete examples of these now survive in Britain.

Sails

The earliest windmill sails were simply rectangular frames comprising a long timber backbone, the whip, through which sail bars were mortised at right angles. The sail frames were double-sided, being the same width on both sides of the whip. Medieval illustrations show that canvas sail cloths were sometimes woven in and out of the bars or spread across the faces of the frames and held in place by cords and ropes. By the sixteenth century, sail frames were being constructed with *weather*, a twist that gave them more driving power, which appears to have originated in the Low Countries. It also became usual to build sails with a narrow frame on the leading edge and a wider frame on the driving side, over which the cloth was spread. Much of the early improvement in the form and construction of windmill sails appears to have been developed empirically by millwrights.

In the mid eighteenth century sail shapes and designs were experimented with in an attempt to improve their power and to provide more control over them in different wind conditions, as it was necessary for a wind miller to stop his mill and set or reef the cloth on each sail by hand. In 1745 Edmund Lee, a smith from Wigan, Lancashire, patented a self-regulating wind machine, which had sails made of boards that could twist and spill the wind if its strength overcame the effect of counterweights connected to the boards by chains. Lee's proposal for self-regulating sails does not appear to have

A medieval post mill, depicted on an early-sixteenth-century bench-end at North Cadbury, Somerset, showing short, wide sails with frames on both sides of the backs or whips.

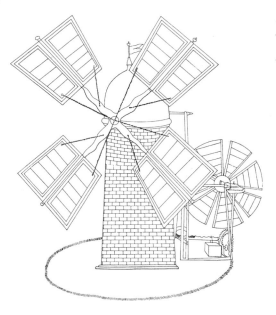

Edmund Lee's self-regulating windmill, from his patent drawing of 1745, is the first representation of shuttered sails and the fantail.

The five-sailed Maud Foster Mill, Boston, Lincolnshire. Built in 1819, the mill is still at work.

The only surviving eight-sailed mill in England, at Heckington, Lincolnshire.

been practical, however. In the 1750s John Smeaton carried out tests using model sails, in order to determine the best shape and angles of weather. He also found that five sails gave more power than the usual four, although there were difficulties fixing an odd number to the end of a timber windshaft, and also problems of balance if one sail was damaged. Smeaton solved this problem by designing a cast-iron cross that was fixed to the outer end of the windshaft, on to which the whips or backs of the frames were secured, the earliest known example being put up on a flint-grinding mill in Leeds in 1774. Many five-sailed mills were subsequently built in northern and eastern England, as well as six-sailers and even a small number with eight sails, of which Heckington Mill, Lincolnshire, which was refitted late in the nineteenth century, is the last surviving example. In England, windmill sails usually revolve in an anti-clockwise direction, when viewed from the front, although there are a number of exceptions that turn clockwise.

The idea of dividing the sail frames into a series of small bays fitted with adjustable shutters that could be controlled remotely appears to have been first proposed by Andrew Meikle, a much respected and ingenious Scottish millwright, who sent a drawing to John Smeaton in

The seventeenth-century post mill at Outwood, Surrey, in working order with four spring sails.

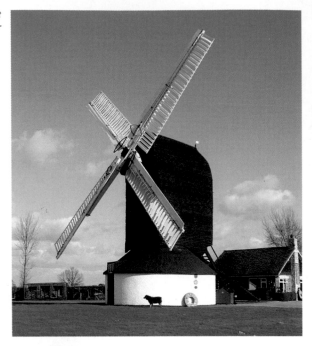

Below: *The distinctive V-shaped air poles controlling the sail shutters on the tower mill at Ballycopeland, County Down, the only surviving example of Stephen Hooper's roller reefing sails.*

the early 1770s. Meikle's idea of controlling the shutters with metal springs does not appear to have been widely adopted until later in the nineteenth century, however. A pair of spring sails was often put up with a pair of common, or cloth-set, sails, to give a practical combination of self-regulation and driving power, mainly on smaller tower mills and post mills.

In 1789 Captain Stephen Hooper, of Margate, Kent, patented what subsequently became known as the roller reefing sail, which comprised a series of small canvas-covered rollers in place of rigid shutters. The rollers on each sail were linked together and could be opened and furled remotely, without stopping the mill. Although invented in Kent, roller reefing sails became most common in East Yorkshire, from where they spread to surrounding areas, largely through the influence of the Hull millwrights Norman & Smithson, who

Fully shuttered sails, after the 1807 patent design of William Cubitt, on the Eastbridge windpump, now in the Museum of East Anglian Life, Stowmarket, Suffolk.

held a licence to use Hooper's patent. No roller reefing sails now survive in England, the only remaining examples being on the restored tower mill at Ballycopeland, County Down.

Although several different forms of self-regulating sail were experimented with between 1789 and 1807, most appear to have had only a short-lived, localised application. William Cubitt's patent of 1807 for self-regulating sails on which the shutters could be controlled remotely became, after some practical modifications, the most successful and widespread sail design to be used in England. Cubitt's sail combined the rigid shutters proposed by Meikle with the control or striking gear modified from Hooper's design, all the shutters on each sail being connected by a rod which in turn was linked by cranks to an iron rod passing through the centre of the windshaft. By moving this rod backwards or forwards, all of the shutters could be opened or closed remotely, without stopping the mill. Weights put on an endless chain that hung down behind or within the mill were used to hold the shutters open when the mill was at rest, or closed when at work, until the strength of the wind overcame their effect, when the shutters would be forced open and spill the wind, and the mill would slow down or stop.

Because of their vulnerability to storm damage and weathering, windmill sails require frequent maintenance and repair, and most of those found on standing and working mills are therefore of recent date. Old photographs and other illustrations provide clear evidence of the

Patent sails on Marsh Mill, Thornton Cleveleys, Lancashire. The distinctive tapering sail tips, once common in mills in north-west England, can be clearly seen.

great variety of shapes and forms that working sails took in different parts of Britain, for example the narrower tips found on windmills in the north-west of England and the thin longitudinal poles on which the sail cloth was rolled or reefed on Somerset mills. Many sails on surviving mills that do not work by wind are flat, shutterless frames, so it is important that local and regional variations in sail design and construction are recorded and, where feasible, restored.

The restored Sarre Mill, Kent, turning with shutters in two of its four patent sails.

A post mill with a roundhouse and tailpole for winding at Mountnessing, Essex.

Winding

Because in northern Europe the wind can blow from any direction, it has always been necessary to build windmills so that their sails can be turned to face squarely into the wind. The earliest method of achieving this was by means of a long lever, the tailpole, which was used on both post and tower mills. Sometimes a cartwheel, which ran around a track laid out around the mill, was fixed to the outer end of the tailpole, or a ring of footholds or timber posts was provided, to give extra purchase for the miller to turn his mill. As tower mills were built taller, it became difficult to use tailpoles and caps were turned by means of a winch. In some mills windlasses and ropes were used, as at Tysoe, Warwickshire, while in others a winch was geared to a ring of cogs projecting from the curb around the top of the tower. In south-west and

Above left: *The ladder and tailpole of the post mill at Stevington, Bedfordshire. Note the short lever, called a talthur, for lifting the ladder clear of the ground when the mill is being turned to wind.*

Above right: *A cartwheel on the end of the tailpole of the Danzey Green post mill, re-erected in the Avoncroft Museum of Buildings, Bromsgrove, Worcestershire, and here at work with two spring and two common sails.*

Below: *Part of the hand winch for turning the cap in the tower mill at Tysoe, Warwickshire.*

The winding gear at the rear of the cap of Stembridge Mill, High Ham, Somerset. An endless rope or chain passing over the wheel to the left enabled the miller to turn the cap through the cast-iron worm which meshes with a gear rack fixed to the curb around the top of the tower wall.

north-west England, caps were usually turned by the miller pulling an endless rope or chain that passed over a grooved wheel connected to the winch at the back of the cap. At Chesterton, Warwickshire, the heavy, large-diameter cap is turned from inside by a double-handed winch geared to a curb with timber cogs around the top of the mill tower.

The automatic winding device known as the fantail first appears applied to a small tower mill in the patent drawing for Edmund Lee's self-regulating wind machine of 1745. This shows a winding wheel, in effect a small set of windmill sails set at right angles to the main sails, by which the cap of the mill was rotated automatically to face the sails into the wind. Lee's idea seems to have been transmitted and first developed in northern England and one of the earliest known representations of its use was on

The restored tower mill at Llynon, Anglesey, showing the winding wheel and chain at the rear of the cap. The timber posts projecting from the tower wall allow the chain to be tied off, to prevent damage in strong winds.

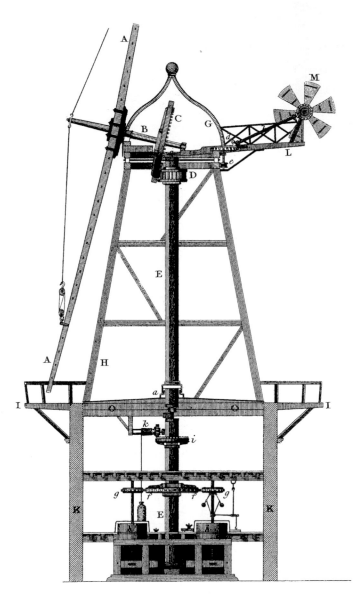

Chimney Mill, Newcastle upon Tyne, from Abraham Rees's 'Cyclopaedia' of 1819. Based on John Smeaton's original design of 1782, this is one of the earliest illustrations of a fantail applied to a tower or smock mill. The principal features are: A, sails; B, windshaft; C, brakewheel; D, wallower; E, upright shaft; G, ogee cap; H, timber-framed body; I, stage; L, fanstage; M, fantail.

John Smeaton's design for Chimney Mill, Newcastle upon Tyne, in 1782. It appears that, along with improvements in sail design and regulation, the fantail found early favour with those entrepreneurs and industrialists who were keen to use new technology, particularly on the larger tower and smock mills that were being built to power industrial processes. The fantail subsequently became one of the most important practical and distinctive additions to many English windmills, particularly in eastern England.

Wilton Mill, near Marlborough, Wiltshire, a brick tower mill built in 1821, now restored with two patent sails, two common sails and a fantail.

Fantails were also fitted to post mills, either high on the back of the mill body, on a framework attached to the tailpole, or on a carriage at the rear of the mill, rather in the manner proposed by Lee. While on tower mills the fantail drove gearing that meshed with a toothed rack on the curb, post-mill fantails were usually geared to a pair of wheels that ran on a track laid out around the base of the mill. The development of shuttered, self-regulating sails and the fantail both depended much on the use of iron for making small gears and, in this respect, windmill development was very much at the forefront of technological progress during the late eighteenth and early nineteenth centuries.

A fantail fixed to the end of the ladder of a post mill at Stanton, Suffolk.

The brakewheel in Cattell's Mill, Willingham, Cambridgeshire, showing a brake made of linked timber blocks, with the brake lever to the lower right.

It is thought that in the Middle Ages windmill sails were stopped by quartering, that is, turning the mill and sails out of the wind. By the end of the fourteenth century a form of brake was in use on windmills in Flanders, and in England the earliest known documentary reference is from Lawling, Essex, in 1526. Windmill brakes are made of linked timber blocks or metal bands which are contracted around the circumference of the headwheel or brakewheel, the primary gear on the windshaft, to slow and stop the mill.

Buttrum's Mill, Woodbridge, Suffolk, built in about 1836, is considered to be one of the finest examples of millwright John Whitmore's work.

*Stembridge Mill,
High Ham,
Somerset, the last
English windmill to
retain a thatched
cap.*

Caps and curbs

The cap forms of both tower and smock mills vary considerably with
region and period. Early illustrations show conical or, possibly, gable-
shaped caps, which enclosed the headwheel or brakewheel and
windshaft. The base of a cap comprises a horizontal frame with two
long timbers, the sheers, with crossbeams between them that support
the neck and tail bearings of the windshaft and the bearing at the head
of the stone spindle or upright shaft. The sheers usually project at the
tail, to carry the winding gear or fantail supports, and the roof of the
cap is framed off them. In south-west England, where caps were
usually thatched, they were gable-shaped and broader at the middle,
with weatherboarded ends. A gable shape with lapped timber
boarding, similar to an upturned boat, was common in north-west

The weatherboarded cap of Woodchurch Mill, Kent, with four patent sails and a fantail.

England and Anglesey, and in south-east England the boarded caps of tower and smock mills are similar in construction to the roofs of post mills. There are several forms of conical cap, domed shapes being found in Cambridgeshire and also West Sussex, but one of the most distinctive forms is the ogee, common on tower mills in the East Midlands, Lincolnshire and the north-east. Many such caps are graced with a finial in the form of a ball and some have a weathervane.

The cap frame rotates on a circular curb, of timber or iron, fixed to the top of the tower wall or smock body. There are several variations in design; in some areas, such as Norfolk and Essex, caps have live

The ogee cap of Skidby Mill, East Yorkshire. Note the red-painted arms of the cast-iron cross carrying the sails.

Looking up into the cap of Denver Mill, Norfolk, showing the underside of the cap circle, curb and truck wheels.

curbs, with rollers fixed to the underside of the frame. The usual form in Lincolnshire is the dead curb, where the cap frame turns on timber or gunmetal blocks, and in Somerset both the surviving tower mills have shot curbs, which comprise an independent ring of evenly spaced rollers set between the timber curb on top of the tower wall and the underside of the cap frame or circle. Caps are usually centred by truck wheels, which are fixed to the underside and run against the inside of the fixed curb around the top of the tower. In Anglesey, the Wirral peninsula and the Fylde district of Lancashire a cap centring or well frame was common, in which angled braces, running from the cap circle down to a horizontal frame at about the level of the top floor of the mill, kept the cap rotation truly circular. Such features are a fascinating part of the development of windmill technology, with local millwrights finding practical solutions to the problems encountered in different parts of Britain.

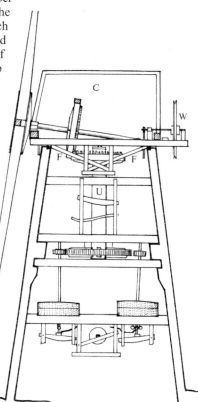

Section through Bidston Mill, Cheshire, showing the cap centring or well frame, F, clasping the top of the upright shaft, U, to keep the rotation of the cap, C, truly circular. W is the winding wheel, for turning the cap.

Machinery

Until the mid eighteenth century, mill gearing was built mostly of timber, with iron used for fastenings and straps and to form bearing surfaces. Iron journals, the bearings fitted to the ends of timber shafts, ran in blocks of stone, bell-metal or even hard wood, usually lubricated with tallow. The earliest type of mill gearing, known as cog and rung, is an uncommon survival in British mills, the brakewheel and wallower of Chesterton Mill, Warwickshire, being rare examples of this early form. Timber gears are usually built of shaped components carried on stout timber arms, with individual wooden cogs inserted into mortises around their working faces. During the eighteenth century the design and construction of millwork underwent considerable change, with the introduction of cast iron. John Smeaton pioneered the use of cast iron for shafts and by the end of the eighteenth century iron was also used for gearing, although initially

Left: The compass-arm brakewheel and lantern wallower in Chesterton Mill, Warwickshire.

Below: The timber brakewheel and wallower in Hickling Mill, Norfolk. Note the slim iron windshaft and the sack-hoist drive taken off an iron gear on the underside of the wallower.

Above: *A fine timber clasp-arm spurwheel driving an iron pinion with wooden cogs in the late-eighteenth-century Sneath's Mill, Lutton, Lincolnshire.*

only for the smaller, driven gears. As ironfounding techniques improved during the nineteenth century, larger gears were cast, although it was usual for them to have timber cogs, which could be fitted and shaped individually to allow for any imperfections in the castings. Wooden cogs meshing with iron teeth also made for quieter running. Later some timber gears had their wooden cogs cut off and cast-iron sections with accurately shaped teeth were bolted in place to form a more durable drive. However, windmills with

Right: *The cast-iron spurwheel above the millstones in the tower mill at North Leverton, Nottinghamshire.*

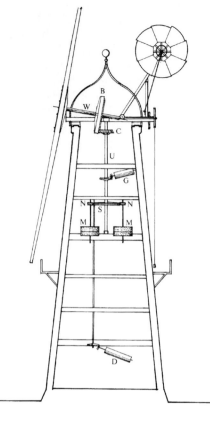

Above: *The restored early-nineteenth-century brick tower mill at Bursledon, Hampshire.*

Right: *A section through Maud Foster Mill, Boston, Lincolnshire, taken from the original 1819 design drawing by the Hull millwrights Norman & Smithson. Note the slim iron shafting and gearing and the planned layout, with a grain cleaner, G, above the millstones, M, and a flour dresser, D, hung below the ground-floor ceiling. W is the windshaft, B the brakewheel, C the crown wheel (wallower), U the upright shaft, S the spurwheel and N the stone nuts.*

timber gearing continued to be built into the nineteenth century, for example at Bursledon, Hampshire (1813–14), and High Ham, Somerset (c.1820). Away from the main areas of windmill development, these smaller tower mills with their common sails and timber gearing provide an interesting contrast with the contemporary tall tower mills with iron machinery being built in Lincolnshire, such as the five-sailed Maud Foster Mill, Boston (1819).

A single pair of millstones driven directly from the brakewheel in Stevington post mill, Bedfordshire.

Corn milling

The majority of windmills of which remains survive in Britain were used for grinding corn, using pairs of horizontal millstones. The earliest windmills had only a single pair of stones, driven directly from the headwheel or brakewheel on the windshaft.

Subsequently gearing was developed to drive two or more pairs of stones, either from above, *overdriven*, or from below, *underdriven*. The confined space in most windmills resulted in relatively cramped conditions at stone-floor level, although in the larger tower mills up to four pairs of stones could be arranged around a vertical shaft. Only the upper stone rotates, the lower being supported on stout beams, with the spindle that supports the upper stone passing through its centre. In underdriven

A pair of millstones overdriven from the spurwheel in Maud Foster Mill, Boston, Lincolnshire.

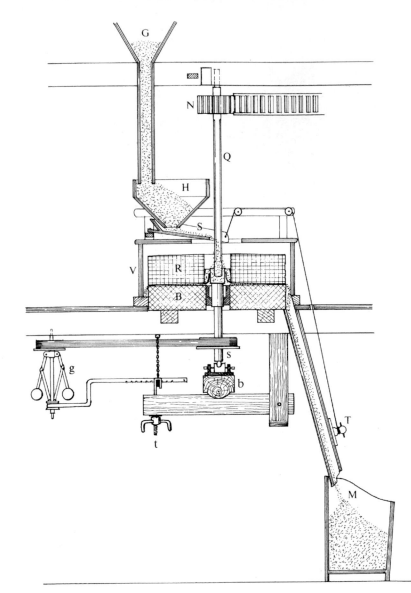

How millstones work. The grain, G, is emptied into a bin and falls by gravity down a spout to the milling hopper, H, from where it is fed into the stones by the shoe, S, which is shaken by the action of the quant, Q. The quant is driven by the stone nut, N, meshing with the spurwheel above the stones. The grain is ground between the faces of the runner stone, R, and the stationary bedstone, B. The vat or tun, V, contains the ground meal as it emerges from between the millstones and falls, by gravity, down the meal spout into the meal bin or ark, M. The amount of grain entering the stones is controlled by adjusting the twist peg and crook string, T, which alters the angle of the shoe. The gap between the stones is set manually by the tentering control, t, which acts through the bridge, b, to raise or lower the spindle, s, and thus the runner stone. The milling gap is maintained automatically by the governor, g, which is driven by belt from the stone spindle, s.

Underdriven millstones in Shade Mill, Soham, Cambridgeshire. Note the governor to the right and the wooden device for lifting the stone nut out of mesh with the spurwheel.

mills the spindle carries the driving gear, the stone nut, and in overdriven mills the stone nut is mounted on a top spindle, the quant. The foot of the spindle runs in a bearing on the bridge tree, or bridge if it is of iron, which is often hung from the beams below the millstones. A further feature of many windmills is a governor, an automatic device that was possibly first introduced in the 1760s. Attached to the tentering or lightering mechanism by which the miller set and controlled the fineness or coarseness of grinding, a governor enabled a consistent texture of ground corn to be produced, even when the wind was gusty.

Grain is hoisted in bags through the mill using the sack hoist, which is usually driven off the brakewheel or the wallower, also known as the crown wheel in some areas, at the head of the upright shaft. It is fed by gravity from hoppers or bins into the milling hopper immediately above the millstones, from where it is directed into the eye, the

Raised sack traps in Trader Mill, Sibsey, Lincolnshire. Continuous hoist chains for lifting several sacks at a time were common in the tall Lincolnshire mills and raising the trap-doors above floor level made handling easier.

Above: *Working millstones in Maud Foster Mill, Boston, Lincolnshire. Grain feeds from the hopper, right, down the inclined timber shoe, which is shaken to and fro by contact with the quant, centre, to fall into the eye of the upper, runner stone.*

Millstone furniture in White Mill, Sandwich, Kent. Behind the millstones, which were driven by an auxiliary engine, is a wire machine, a form of dresser for separating various grades of flour.

Above left: *Spouts and bins in Pakenham Mill, Suffolk, where the ground meal was collected from the millstones on the floor above.*

Above right: *The miller's tools: sack trucks and scales for moving and weighing grain and meal in Pakenham Mill, Suffolk.*

Below: *A bolter, for separating fine flour, squeezed in below the beam carrying the tail bearing of the windshaft in Aythorpe Roding post mill, Essex.*

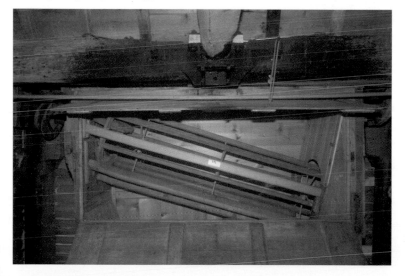

A sack hoist driven by belt from the windshaft in the roof of Mountnessing post mill, Essex. The control lever for tensioning the belt is to the right.

centre of the runner stone, to be ground between the faces of the two stones. The ground corn, or meal, falls down a spout to be bagged up on the floor below. In addition to millstones, many windmills have machines for cleaning the grain before it is milled and for dressing flour – separating the fine whiter flour from the coarser particles and bran. In some post mills there are clear signs that the mill body had to be extended to allow a flour dresser to be fitted.

The post mill at Saxtead Green, Suffolk, now in the care of English Heritage.

Drainage mills

In the Netherlands wind power was used from the fourteenth century to drive scoop wheels for lifting water in land reclamation schemes. A scoop wheel is similar in design to a waterwheel but is turned by the sails of the windmill to raise water from a lower to a higher level. The earliest form of drainage windmill was probably the hollow-post mill, but smock mills were introduced by the sixteenth century. Drainage mills often worked in gangs, each one lifting water only 1.5 metres or so. In the English Fenland windmills were introduced by the middle of the sixteenth century in order to drain land but, unlike in the Netherlands, they were often sited to lift water into rivers that were liable to flood, or into tidal reaches where water levels were constantly changing, so they were frequently unable to work. Fenland windmills were timber-framed smock mills, usually vertically boarded, with four common sails and tailpole winding. Only one small example still

A re-erected scoop wheel from a drainage mill, at Repps, near Great Yarmouth, Norfolk.

Above: *Casing enclosing a scoop wheel, with the drive shaft entering from the left, at High Mill, Berney Arms, Norfolk.*

The last fen drainage mill at Wicken Fen, Cambridgeshire.

The re-erected Eastbridge windpump at the Museum of East Anglian Life, Stowmarket, Suffolk. Built in the mid nineteenth century, it was one of four windpumps used to drain Minsmere Level, near Leiston, and was rescued by Suffolk Mills Group volunteers in 1977.

Right: *A section through a typical small Norfolk drainage mill driving a scoop wheel, S.*

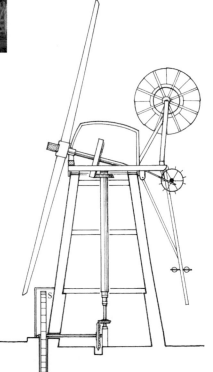

survives, at Wicken Fen in Cambridgeshire, where conversely it is now used occasionally to keep the fen wet, for conservation purposes, rather than to drain it.

While arable farming was important in the Fens, grass for grazing was the principal crop in the Norfolk Broads area and here drainage windmills survived in use longer than elsewhere. Timber smock mills appear to have been the earliest form used, the mill at Herringfleet, Suffolk, which was built in 1830, being a later example. Brick tower mills were also in use by the middle of the eighteenth century, originally driving scoop wheels, but from the 1850s the Appold centrifugal pump began to supersede them.

Turf Fen Mill, Barton Turf, Norfolk, a small drainage mill on the River Ant, restored by the Norfolk Windmills Trust.

Below left: *The casing and drive of the turbine pump at Thurne Dyke drainage mill, Norfolk.*

Below right: *Clayrack Pump, How Hill, Ludham, Norfolk, a small hollow-post drainage mill, which formerly stood at Ranworth Broad, was moved to its present position in the 1980s and is now restored.*

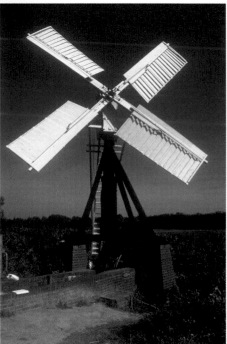

A small mid-nineteenth-century hollow-post windpump, originally at Westham, near Pevensey, now rebuilt at the Weald & Downland Museum, Singleton, West Sussex.

The last Norfolk drainage mill, at Ashtree Farm, stopped work in 1953, although a number of drainage mills and some smaller windpumps have been restored. A fine example is High Mill at Berney Arms, a tall brick tower mill with four patent sails and a fantail, which, in addition to pumping water by scoop wheel, drove machinery for grinding cement clinker, made from mud dredged from the river.

Industrial and agricultural windmills

The oldest use of wind power in Britain, other than for grinding corn or pumping water, was for crushing seeds for extracting oil, possibly as early as the fourteenth century. Oil-bearing seeds such as linseed and rapeseed were crushed using vertical millstones known as edge runners to extract oil, which was used for lighting, wool treatment and lubrication and, later, in soap and paint manufacture. A smock mill for crushing oilseed was built in King's Lynn, Norfolk, in 1638, and it is thought that the frame of the mill was brought over from the Netherlands. In the district around Hull, East Yorkshire, where the potential for water power was small, windmills were used to produce oil and also to drive a variety of industrial processes, including timber

Left: *The remains of the last wind-driven oil mill in England, at Hawkestone, Weston, Shropshire. The brick tower mill probably dates from the 1780s.*

Below: *The early-nineteenth-century brick tower mill at Hessle, near Hull, East Yorkshire, was built to grind chalk for whiting, used in the production of putty and paint.*

Parys Mountain, Anglesey: the tower of the windmill built in 1878 to assist a steam engine that pumped water and raised ore from a copper mine. The mill, which had five sails, was out of use by 1910.

sawing, papermaking, and grinding chalk for whiting, which was used in making paint. Wind power was also used in the non-ferrous metal industries, for pumping water from mines, as at the Parys Mountain copper mine on Anglesey, and grinding minerals. At Warmley, near Bristol, the tall stone tower of a windmill built in the mid eighteenth century to crush calamine, which was used in the production of brass, survives on the site of William Champion's former brass works. Not far away, overlooking the Avon gorge

Below left: *The tower of a windmill built in the mid eighteenth century to pump water and crush calamine, for brass-making, at Warmley, near Bristol.*

Below right: *Clifton Observatory, Bristol. The tower of this windmill, built originally to grind snuff, now houses a camera obscura.*

A former threshing windmill, built alongside a barn and a horse wheelhouse at Shortrigg, Hoddam, Dumfries and Galloway.

in Bristol, stands the tower of a windmill that was built as a corn mill in 1767 and converted to grind snuff before being burnt out in a gale ten years later.

The first successful threshing machine was patented by Andrew Meikle, the East Lothian millwright, in 1788 and from the late eighteenth century some tower mills were built, particularly in Scotland and the north of England, to drive threshers and other barn machines. Such windmills were uncommon elsewhere, but in about 1820 a six-sided smock mill was built at West Blatchington, East Sussex, on top of a barn that housed two pairs of millstones, a threshing machine and other farm machinery.

The six-sided smock mill built on top of a barn at West Blatchington, East Sussex, c.1820.

The peak of English windmill technology: the five-sailed mill at Alford, Lincolnshire, which dates from the 1830s.

Heyday and decline

Corn milling was always the principal function of the windmill in Britain and at the end of the eighteenth century, when water-power sites were in great demand for textile and other processing industries, the milling industry came to rely more and more on wind power. The decline of windmilling was speeded by the development of less fickle sources of power, such as improved waterwheels and steam engines, and the failure of the wind to blow steadily during working hours. The English windmill probably reached its peak of development during the second and third decades of the nineteenth century, held that peak for a brief period, and then declined, although new windmills were still being built during the last quarter of the nineteenth century. During the

Above: *Everton, Nottinghamshire: the derelict tower of a corn-grinding windmill, dating from c.1820, stands beside the remains of a steam mill that was built in 1898 and worked into the 1940s.*

Left: *An early type of roller mill, with porcelain rolls, which worked alongside millstones in the windmill at Whissendine, Rutland.*

Below: *Landmark from a vanished age: the remains of a vaulted stone tower mill at Balgone Barns, East Lothian, with Traprain Law in the background.*

A derelict tower mill at Great Haseley, Oxfordshire. There is still a small number of windmills that have not been highlighted for preservation and repair.

1870s new technology in the form of iron roller mills began to replace millstones in the production of flour, and windmills were the first to lose trade to the new steam mills that were being built in many major ports. Although auxiliary engines were introduced to turn the machinery on windless days, by the end of the nineteenth century many windmills had stopped work and, because of the vulnerability of the sails and superstructure to storm damage and decay, many soon disappeared from the landscape.

Preservation

The windmill preservation movement started before the end of the nineteenth century, for the hollow-post mill on Wimbledon Common was restored, albeit in an altered form, in 1893, and Bidston Mill, on the Wirral peninsula, was restored as a landmark a year later. But the number of working windmills declined rapidly and in 1929 the Society for the Protection of Ancient Buildings (SPAB), the oldest building conservation society in the world, launched a campaign to protect those windmills that survived. Many more mills stopped work during the 1930s, however, and some were gutted of their iron machinery during the Second World War. In the late 1940s windmills were going out of use at the rate of about one a month and by 1951 it was estimated that only about ten per cent of the windmills that were active in 1924

Left: *The ravages of time: remains of the machinery surviving in the tower of Gilmorton Mill, Leicestershire, in the early 1980s.*

Below: *The stone floor of Mountnessing Mill, Essex. Restored by Essex County Council in 1983, this post mill, like many others, is worked occasionally by volunteer millers.*

Repairs to the roof of the post mill from Windmill Hill, Herstmonceux, East Sussex, being undertaken in the workshops of IJP Building Conservation Ltd, at Henley-on-Thames, Oxfordshire.

were still at work. During the 1960s and 1970s many windmills were targeted for preservation, and work carried out by sympathetic owners, amateur enthusiasts, professional millwrights and conservation bodies such as the National Trust and English Heritage has ensured the continued survival of some important examples. The Mills Section of

The fate of many windmills: a house converted from a former tower mill at Saredon, Staffordshire. There are many worse examples.

The restored tower mill at Denver, Norfolk. Built in 1835, the mill has been restored to working order and produces wholemeal flour.

the SPAB has carried forward the co-ordination of work to protect, conserve and maintain both windmills and watermills into the twenty-first century and, while it is gratifying to record that in 2005 over 140 restored windmills were open to the public, these survivors are but a small proportion of the thousands of windmills, each one individual in some way, that once raised their sails above the rooftops of many towns and graced a wide variety of British landscapes.

Below: *Skidby Mill, East Yorkshire, one of the last working windmills north of the River Humber, is located only a few miles from the site of one of the earliest recorded English windmills.*

Glossary

Bearing: the static part of a machine in which a journal runs.

Brakewheel: the primary gear mounted on the windshaft in windmills, on which the brake acts.

Clasp arm: a form of construction used for gear wheels where two pairs of arms form a square at the centre that boxes the shaft on to which the wheel is fixed.

Cog: an individual timber tooth inserted into a gearwheel.

Common sail: the earliest form of windmill sail where cloth is spread over a lattice framework.

Compass arm: a form of construction in which the arms of a gear are mortised through the shaft.

Crosstrees: the main horizontal timbers of the trestle of a post mill, from which the quarterbars rise to support the post.

Crown wheel: a horizontal-face gear, with its cogs or teeth usually projecting upwards, from which drives are taken by pinions and layshafts.

Dressing: the art of preparing the working faces of millstones for grinding. Also used for sieving meal to make a finer flour.

Edge runner stones: a pair of vertically mounted stones that rotate on a fixed horizontal bedstone, used for crushing rather than grinding.

Eye: the hole through the centre of a millstone.

Fantail: a small wind wheel set at right angles to the sails of a windmill to turn the mill automatically into the wind.

Governor: a device for controlling the gap between millstones.

Grindstone: a single, vertically mounted rotating stone used for sharpening tools.

Harps: a pattern of furrows laid out in triangular segments on the working face of a millstone.

Head and tail: the arrangement of two gearwheels mounted one behind the other on the windshaft of a post mill, from which drives to millstones are taken.

Hollow-post mill: a post mill in which the drive is taken down to the base of the mill by a vertical shaft passing through the hollowed centre of the post.

Horizontal windmill: a type of windmill in which the sails rotate in a horizontal plane.

Hurst: the sturdy timber frame that supports the millstones in a corn mill.

Journal: circular part of a shaft, usually of metal, which runs in a bearing.

Lantern pinion: a driven gear formed of two discs with staves between, which serve as cogs.

Millstone: one of a pair of usually horizontal stones for grinding corn.

Millwright: traditionally, someone who builds and maintains mills.

Overdriven: machinery, particularly millstones, driven from above.

Patent sail: a form of remotely regulated shutter sail patented in 1807.

Pinion: the smaller wheel of two wheels in gear, and driven by the larger wheel. Sometimes referred to as a nut.

Poll end/canister: the outer end of a windshaft, to which the sails are attached.

Post mill: a timber-framed mill of which the body, containing the machinery and carrying the sails, rotates about the head of a massive vertical post.

Quarterbars: the raking struts rising from the crosstrees that support the post of a post mill.

Roller mill: a machine with cylindrical rollers for crushing grain or other raw materials. Also a type of mill developed during the nineteenth century in which a series of rolls in combination with sieves is used to produce fine flour.

Roller reefing sail: a form of remote-controlled shuttered sail patented in 1789.

Runner: the upper moving stone of a pair of millstones.

Rynd: an iron fitting on which the upper, moving millstone is hung.

Sail bars: the short lateral bars of a windmill sail.

Scoop wheel: a driven wheel used to raise water in land drainage.

Shuttered sail: a form of windmill sail which is divided into a series of bays filled with movable shutters.

Smock mill: a timber-framed tower windmill, in England usually clad with horizontal or vertical timber boarding.

Spider: the cranks at the centre of a set of patent sails which link the shutters to the striking rod.

Spindle: a small-diameter shaft, usually of iron.

Spring sail: the earliest form of shuttered sail, in which the shutters were held closed by tensioned springs.

Spurwheel drive: a gearing form in which a number of drives can be taken off the periphery of a spur gear. In a windmill the spurwheel is horizontal and a number of pairs of millstones can be grouped around a central shaft.

Striking rod: a rod passing through the centre of a windshaft, which connects the shutters of patent sails to the striking gear, by which the shutters are remotely controlled.

Tailpole: a beam at the bottom of a post-mill body or extending from the cap of a tower mill used to turn the mill to the wind.

Tailwheel: in a post mill, a gear wheel mounted towards the inner end of the windshaft that drives millstones located in the tail of the mill.

Threshing machine: a farm machine used for separating grain from straw and chaff after harvesting.

Tower mill: a windmill comprising a masonry tower containing the machinery and a rotating cap at the top carrying the windshaft and sails.

Trestle: the substructure of a post mill.

Underdriven: machinery, particularly millstones, driven from below.

Wallower: the first gear driven by the pitwheel in a watermill and the brakewheel in a windmill.

Weather: the twist of a windmill sail to the plane of rotation, necessary to transform the wind's energy into motive power.

Windshaft: the main driveshaft in a windmill that carries the sails at its outer end and is turned by them.

Finchingfield Mill, Essex, a small post mill dating from about 1756, is owned and maintained by Essex County Council.

Further reading

GENERAL
de Little, Rodney. *The Windmills of England.* Colwood Press, 1997. An enthusiast's book, with much interesting background to windmill preservation and repair.
Freese, Stanley. *Windmills and Millwrighting.* Cambridge University Press, 1957; reprinted David & Charles, 1971. A classic, written by one of the first generation of windmill enthusiasts.
Gregory, Roy. *The Industrial Windmill in Britain.* Phillimore, 2005. Gives good breadth to the subject, with useful discussion of eighteenth-century windmill technology.
Hills, Richard. *Power from Wind.* Cambridge University Press, 1994. Covers British and European windmills, with information on patents of invention and on land drainage.
Holt, Richard. *The Mills of Medieval England.* Blackwell, 1988.
Langdon, John. *Mills in the Medieval Economy.* Oxford University Press, 2004.
These two academic works present a balanced overall view of the technical development of mills and their role in medieval society.
Reynolds, John. *Windmills and Watermills.* Evelyn, 1970. Provides good general background, with excellent drawings.
Wailes, Rex. *The English Windmill.* Routledge & Keegan Paul, 1954, and subsequent editions. This still stands as the classic study of English windmills, written by an engineer with a broad knowledge of windmills.
Watts, Martin. *Water and Wind Power.* Shire, 2000; reprinted 2005. A general survey, setting the history and technical development of windmills alongside that of watermills.

LOCAL STUDIES
There are many county studies and gazetteers, almost every English county having been covered at some time, some more than once. A small selection is:
Apling, Harry. *Norfolk Corn Windmills.* Norfolk Windmills Trust, 1984.
Brunnarius, Martin. *The Windmills of Sussex.* Phillimore, 1979.
Coulthard, Alfred J., and Watts, Martin. *Windmills of Somerset.* Research Publishing Co, 1978.
Dolman, Peter. *Lincolnshire Windmills.* Lincolnshire County Council, 1986.
Douglas, G.; Oglethorpe, M.; and Hume, J. R. *Scottish Windmills: A Survey.* Scottish Industrial Archaeology Survey, 1984.
Farries, Kenneth. *Essex Windmills, Millers and Millwrights* (five volumes). Charles Skilton, 1981–8.
Flint, Brian. *Suffolk Windmills.* Boydell, 1979.
Gregory, Roy. *East Yorkshire Windmills.* Charles Skilton, 1985.
Guise, Barry, and Lees, George. *Windmills of Anglesey.* Attic Books, 1992.
Harrison, John K. *Eight Centuries of Milling in North East Yorkshire.* North York Moors National Park Authority, 2001.
Job, Barry. *Staffordshire Windmills.* Midland Wind and Watermills Group, 1984.
Moon, Nigel. *Leicestershire and Rutland Windmills.* Daedalus Press, 1981.
Watts, Martin. *Wiltshire Windmills.* Wiltshire County Council, 1980.
West, Jenny. *The Windmills of Kent.* Skilton & Shaw, 1979.

There are also numerous guide books and histories of individual mills. Much detailed and useful information can be found in local history and archaeology society journals, as well as the newsletters and journals of the local and regional mill groups that now cover many parts of England and Wales. Details of these groups and other activities concerned with the study, preservation and maintenance of Britain's milling heritage can be obtained from The Mills Section, Society for the Protection of Ancient Buildings, 37 Spital Square, London E1 6DY; telephone: 020 7456 0909; website: www.spab.org.uk A valuable resource with a growing body of information and pictures of traditional mills is The Mills Archive, Watlington House, 44 Watlington Street, Reading RG1 4RJ; website: www.millsarchive.com

Windmills to visit

The following windmills are generally accessible to the public, although it is advisable to check opening arrangements in advance, particularly if travelling some distance, as some of the mills listed are open by appointment only. There are numerous other examples and remains to be found scattered around the British countryside, but private ownership and the country code should be respected when seeking access to such sites.

(P) = post mill; (S) = smock mill; (T) = tower mill.

Many mills have their own websites and there is also a number of general websites worth visiting that belong to windmill societies and groups:
www. kentwindmills.homestead.com
www.lincolnshire.gov.uk (under places to visit) and www.lincolnshire.gov.uk/windmills
www.midlandmills.org.uk
www.norfolkwindmills.co.uk
www.suffolkmills.org.uk
www.sussexmillsgroup.org.uk

Bedfordshire
Stevington Mill (P), Stevington, Bedford. Telephone: 01234 824330. Website: www.bedfordshire.gov.uk

Buckinghamshire
Lacey Green Mill (S), Lacey Green, near Princes Risborough. Telephone: 01844 343560. Website:
    www.chilternsociety.org.uk
Pitstone Mill (P), Ivinghoe. Telephone: 01442 851227. Website: www.nationaltrust.org.uk
Quainton Mill (T), Quainton, Aylesbury. Telephone: 01296 655348. Website: www.quainton.net

Cambridgeshire
Bourn Mill (P), Bourn, Cambridge. Telephone: 01223 243830. Website: www.cpswandlebury.org
Cattell's Mill (S), Willingham. Telephone: 01954 261168.

The fine smock mill at Wicken, Cambridgeshire, taken during repainting of the cap and fantail in 2003.

Fulbourn Mill, Cambridgeshire. Built in 1808, this smock mill is maintained and opened by the Fulbourn Windmill Society.

Chishill Mill (P), Great Chishill. Telephone: 01763 837263.
Foster's Mill (T), Swaffham Prior. Telephone: 01638 741009. Website: www.fostersmill.co.uk
Fulbourn Mill (S), Fulbourn. Telephone: 01223 880649. Website: www.fulbourn.windmill.btinternet.co.uk
Great Gransden Mill (P), Mill Road, Great Gransden. Telephone: 01767 677487.
Impington Mill (S), Cambridge Road, Impington, Cambridge. Telephone: 01223 232284. (Private residence, visits by prior appointment only)
Madingley Mill (P), Madingley. Telephone: 01954 211047. (By prior appointment only)
Over Mill (T), Over. Telephone: 01954 230742. (By prior appointment only)
Stevens Mill (T), Burwell. Telephone: 01638 605544. Website: www.burwellmuseum.org.uk
Wicken Fen Pumping Mill (S), Wicken Fen Nature Reserve. Telephone: 01353 720274. Website: www.wicken.org.uk
Wicken Mill (S), Wicken. Telephone: 01664 822751. Website: www.geocities.com/wickenmill

Derbyshire
Heage Mill (T), Belper. Telephone: 01773 853579. Website: www.heagewindmill.co.uk

County Durham
Fulwell Mill (T), Newcastle Road, Fulwell, Sunderland. Telephone: 0191 516 9790. Website: www.fulwell-windmill.com

Essex
Aythorpe Roding Mill (P), near Leaden Roding. Telephone: 01245 437663 or 07887 662177. Website: www.essexcc.gov.uk
Bocking Mill (P), off Church Street, Bocking. Telephone: 01376 324781. Website: http://beehive.thisisessex.co.uk
Finchingfield Mill (P), Haverhill Road, Finchingfield. Telephone: 01245 437663 or 07887 662177. Website: www.essexcc.gov.uk
John Webb's Mill (T), Thaxted, Dunmow. Telephone: 01371 830285.
Mountnessing Mill (P), near Brentwood. Telephone: 01245 437663 or 07887 662177. Website: www.essexcc.gov.uk
Stansted Mountfitchet Mill (T), Millside, Stansted Mountfitchet. Telephone: 01279 647213.

Bembridge Mill, Isle of Wight.

Stock Mill (T), Mill Lane, Stock, Chelmsford.
   Telephone: 01245 437663 or 07887 662177. Website:
   www.essexcc.gov.uk
Upminster Mill (S). Telephone: 01708 226040. Website:
   www.upminsterwindmill.co.uk

Hampshire
Bursledon Mill (T), Windmill Lane, Bursledon.
   Telephone: 023 8040 4999. Website:
   www.hants.gov.uk/museum/windmill

Hertfordshire
Cromer Mill (P), near Stevenage. Telephone: 01279
   843301. Website: www.hertsmuseums.org.uk/cromer-
   windmill

Isle of Wight
Bembridge Mill (T), High Street, Bembridge. Telephone:
   01983 873945. Website: www.nationaltrust.org.uk

Kent
Draper's Mill (S), St Peter's Footpath, off College Road,
   Margate. Telephone: 01843 226227 or 291696.
Herne Mill (S), Mill View Road, Herne. Telephone:
   01227 361326.
Meopham Mill (S), Meopham Green. Telephone: 01474
   813518 or 812794.
Sarre Mill (S), Canterbury Road, Sarre. Telephone: 01843 847573.
Stelling Minnis Mill (S), Canterbury. Telephone: 01227 709550 or 709238.
   Website: www.stelling-minnis.co.uk/windmill
Stock's Mill (P), Wittersham. Telephone: 01797 270295.
Union Mill (S), The Hill, Cranbrook. Telephone: 01580 712984 or 712256.
   Website: http://tonysing.orpheusweb.co.uk/Union
White Mill (S), Sandwich. Telephone: 01304 612076. Website: http://whitemill.open-sandwich.co.uk
Willesborough Mill (S), Ashford. Telephone: 01233 661866.
   Website: www.willesboroughwindmill.co.uk
Woodchurch Mill (S), Tenterden. Telephone: 01233 860649.
   Website: www.woodchurchwindmill.co.uk

Lancashire
Lytham Mill (T), Lytham St Annes. Telephone: 01253 725610 (all year) or 794879 (seasonal). Website:
   www.lythamheritage.fsnet.co.uk/lytham_windmill.htm
Marsh Mill (T), Thornton Cleveleys, Blackpool. Telephone: 01253 860765. Website: www.wyrebc.gov.uk

Leicestershire
Hough Mill (T), off St George's Hill, Swannington. Telephone: 01530 832704. Website: www.swannington-
   heritage.co.uk
Wymondham Mill (T), Wymondham. Telephone: 01572 787304.
   Website: www.wymondhamwindmill.co.uk

Lincolnshire
Alford Mill (T), Mablethorpe Road, Alford. Telephone: 01507 462136.
   Website: www.alfordtown.co.uk/shared/mill/mill.htm
Dobson's Mill (T), High Street, Burgh le Marsh. Telephone: 01754 810324.
   Website: www.burghlemarsh.info/windmill
Ellis's Mill (T), Mill Road, Lincoln. Telephone: 01522 528448.
Heckington Mill (T), Heckington, Sleaford. Telephone: 01529 461919.
Hewitt's Windmill (T), Heapham, Gainsborough. Telephone: 01427 838230. (Most days by appointment)
Maud Foster Mill (T), Willoughby Road, Boston. Telephone: 01205 352188.
Moulton Mill (T), Moulton, Spalding. Telephone: 01406 373237.

Above left: *The restored smock mill at Woodchurch, Kent, built c.1820.*
Above right: *Ellis's Mill, Lincoln.*

Mount Pleasant Mill (T), North Cliff Road, Kirton-in-Lindsey. Telephone: 01652 640177.
　　Website: www.mountpleasantwindmill.co.uk
Trader Mill (T), Sibsey, Boston. Telephone: 01205 750036.
Waltham Mill (T), Brigsley Road, Waltham. Telephone: 01472 752122. Website:
　　www.walthamwindmill.co.uk
Wrawby Mill (P), Wrawby, Brigg. Telephone: 01652 653699.

London
Wimbledon Mill (S), Wimbledon Common, London. Telephone: 020 8947 2825.
　　Website: www.wimbledonwindmillmuseum.org.uk

Norfolk
Berney Arms Mill (T), Great Yarmouth. Telephone: 01223 582700 or 01493 700605.
　　Website: www.english-heritage.org.uk
Billingford Mill (T), Billingford. Telephone: 01603 222705.
Boardman's and Clayrack Drainage Mills, How Hill, Ludham. Telephone: 01603 222705.
Denver Mill (T), Downham Market. Telephone: 01366 384009. Website: www.denvermill.co.uk
Garboldisham Mill (P), Garboldisham. Telephone: 01953 681593.
Great Bircham Mill (T), Great Bircham, King's Lynn. Telephone: 01485 578393.
　　Website: www.birchamwindmill.co.uk
Horsey Windpump (T), Potter Heigham. Telephone: 01493 393904.
　　Website: www.nationaltrust.org.uk
Little Cressingham Wind and Watermill (T), Watton. Telephone: 01603 222705.
Old Buckenham Corn Mill (T), Attleborough. Telephone: 01603 222705.
Stracey Arms Drainage Mill (T), Acle. Telephone: 01603 222705.
Thurne Dyke Drainage Mill (T). Telephone: 01603 222705.
Wicklewood Mill (T), Wymondham. Telephone: 01603 222705.

The Midlands-type post mill at Wrawby, Lincolnshire.

Nottinghamshire
Green's Mill (T), Windmill Lane, Sneinton, Nottingham. Telephone: 0115 915 6878.
    Website: www.greensmill.org.uk
North Leverton Mill (T), Mill Lane, North Leverton, Retford. Telephone: 01427 880439, 880662 or
    880923.
Tuxford Mill (T), Tuxford. Telephone: 01777 871202.

Oxfordshire
Chinnor Mill (P), Mill Lane, Chinnor. Telephone: 01844 292095. Website:
    www.chinnorparishcouncil.org.uk
Wheatley Mill (T), Windmill Lane, Wheatley. Telephone: 01865 874610.
    Website: http://www.advsys.co.uk/wheatleymill

Rutland
Whissendine Mill (T), Melton Road, Whissendine. Telephone: 01664 474172. (By appointment only)

Shropshire
Asterley Mill (T), Minsterley. Telephone: 01743 791434. (By appointment only)

Somerset
Ashton Mill (T), Chapel Allerton, Wedmore. Telephone: 01278 435399.
    Website: www.somerset.gov.uk/celebratingsomerset
Stembridge Mill (T), High Ham, Langport TA10 9DJ. Telephone: 01458 250818.
    Website: www.nationaltrust.org.uk

Staffordshire
Broad Eye Mill (T), Castle Hill, Stafford. Telephone: 01785 613558.
    Website: http://website.lineone.net/~broadeyewindmill

Suffolk
Bardwell Mill (T), Bardwell, Ixworth. Telephone: 01359 251331.
Buttrum's Mill (T), Woodbridge. Telephone: 01473 264755. Website: www.tidemill.org.uk/buttmill.html
Drinkstone Mills (P and S), Bury St Edmunds. Telephone: 07843 074700.
Eastbridge Windpump (S), Museum of East Anglian Life, Stowmarket IP14 1DL. Telephone: 01449
    612229. Website: http://www.eastanglianlife.org.uk

Herringfleet Windpump (S), Somerleyton, Lowestoft. Telephone: 01473 264755.
Pakenham Mill (T), Bury St Edmunds. Telephone: 01359 230277.
Saxtead Green Mill (P), Framlingham. Telephone: 01728 685789.
 Website: www.english-heritage.org.uk
Stanton Mill (P), Upthorpe Road, Stanton, Bury St Edmunds. Telephone: 01359 250622.
 Website: www.stantonwindmill.members.beeb.net Email: stantonwindmill@hotmail.com
Thelnetham Mill (T), Mill Lane, Thelnetham. Telephone: 01473 727853 or 264755.

Surrey
Buckland Mill (S), Dungates Lane, Betchworth. Telephone: 01737 843388.
 Website: www.bucklandsurrey.net
Outwood Mill (P), Outwood Common, near Redhill. Telephone: 01342 843458.
Shirley Mill (T), Post Mill Close, Shirley, Croydon. Telephone: 020 8406 4676.
 Website: www.croydon.gov.uk/leisure/artsentertainment/culture

Sussex, East
Nutley Mill (P), Crowborough Road, Nutley, Uckfield. Telephone: 01435 873367.
 Website: www.udps.co.uk
Polegate Mill (T), Park Croft, Polegate. Telephone: 01323 734496.
 Website: www.sussexmillsgroup.org.uk
Stone Cross Mill (T), Stone Cross. Telephone: 01323 763206 or 763253.
West Blatchington Mill (S), Holmes Avenue, Hove. Telephone: 01273 776017.

Sussex, West
High Salvington Mill (P), Worthing. Telephone: 01903 262443.
 Website: www.highsalvingtonwindmill.co.uk
Jill Mill (P), Clayton. Website: www.jillwindmill.org.uk Email: jillwindmill@hotmail.com
Lowfield Heath Mill (P), Rusper Road, Lowfield Heath. Telephone: 01293 862374.
Oldland Mill (P), Keymer. Telephone: 01273 842342. Website: www.oldlandwindmill.co.uk
Pevensey Windpump (P), Weald & Downland Open Air Museum, Singleton, Chichester PO18 0EU.
 Telephone: 01243 811363. Website: http://www.wealddown.co.uk
Shipley Mill (S), near Horsham. Telephone: 01403 730439. Website: www.shipleywindmill.org.uk

Warwickshire
Chesterton Mill (T), Chesterton, Warwick. Telephone: 01926 412500.
 Website: www.warwickshire.gov.uk
Tysoe Mill (T), Compton Wynyates. (Can be viewed from public footpath; interior very rarely opened to the
 public except on special occasions)

Wiltshire
Wilton Mill (T), Wilton, Marlborough. Telephone: 01672 870202.
 Website: www.wiltonwindmill.co.uk

Worcestershire
Danzey Green Mill (P), Avoncroft Museum of Buildings, Stoke Heath, Bromsgrove B60 4JR. Telephone:
 01527 831363 or 831886. Website: www.avoncroft.org.uk

Yorkshire, East
Hessle Mill (T), Cliffe Road, Hessle. Telephone: 01482 392773.
Skidby Mill (T), Cottingham. Telephone: 01482 392773.

Yorkshire, North
Elvington Brickyard Windpump (T), Elvington Lake Cottage, Elvington YO41 4AZ. Telephone: 01904
 608255.

Wales
Melin Llynon (T), Llanddeusant, Anglesey. Telephone: 01407 730797.
 Website: www.anglesey.gov.uk

Northern Ireland
Ballycopeland Mill (T), Millisle, Newtownards, County Down. Telephone: 028 9054 6552.
 Website: www.ehsni.gov.uk/places/monuments/ballycopeland.shtml

Index

Page numbers in italics refer to illustrations